EMOTIONALAGILITY:

How to develop communication skills without stress.
Book 2

Anne Gilmore

2017

Copyright 2017 © by Anne Gilmore
All rights reserved.
ISBN-13: 978-1979263894
ISBN-10: 1979263892

Contents

Introduction — 4
Communication Skills — 4

Chapter 1
Benefits of emotional intelligence — 5

Chapter 2
How Emotional quotient effects emotional intelligence — 7
Increasing your EQ — 8

Chapter 3
Developing emotional intelligence in the Workplace — 15
Employee Assessments — 18

Chapter 4
Awareness and understanding of the emotions of others. — 21
Empathy- Practice Empathizing with Yourself and Others — 21
Examine How Your Actions Will Affect Others — 22
Practice Responding, Rather Than Reacting — 23
Types of People and How to Handle Them — 25

Chapter 5
Managing the emotions of others — 27
How Does EQ Work in Relationships? — 27
What Happens If You Don't Have a Well Developed EQ? — 27
Can EQ Be Taught? — 28
EQ At Home 1 – Couples — 28
EQ at Home (Parents) — 30
EQ at Your Workplace (Social Responsibility) — 31

Chapter 6
Tips & Tricks to Improve Your Emotional Intelligence — 33

Conclusion — 39

Introduction

Communication Skills

Communicating is the #1 life skill you'll need to get the most of out of your life. The world revolves around our ability to communicate with one another. Developing this skill will help every aspect of your life, from social to professional. It's never too late to begin. By definition, communication is "the act of exchanging information from one spot to another, either by voice, the written word, nonverbal cues, or visual aid." How good a job we do at transmitting and receiving this information is a measure of our skill in communicating.

People with high EQ are deft at not only expressing their feelings but recognizing how those around them feel. It's important to master each of the below skills as they will all work together to allow you to communicate more efficiently on the whole.

Chapter 1
Benefits of emotional intelligence

Feelings and emotions are far from effects which just occur in your life. You may falsely judge the sense of anxiety, annoyance, melancholy, love, dislike, happiness, excitement among other sentiments, which can, in turn, alter the way you react to the world around you. Studies have shown that emotional intelligence in high levels is extremely advantageous to increase the value of life. It would then give life a never-ending assessment.

Here Are Several Advantages Of Emotional Intelligence:

1) Stress Management

Stress is a case of psychological pressure that stems from conflicting circumstances. Anyone and everyone deal with some types of stress throughout their lives. The ability to cope with stress is how well you can tolerate these unfavorable aspects. Those with a high level of emotional intelligence can endure the hardships that life has to offer with confidence and high self-esteem. They remain stable and steady in the face of powerful emotions and feelings.

2) Self-Control

Self-control is a different emotion which allows you to postpone gratification for a period to achieve greater results. Restraint is a delicate balance and characteristic of the willingness to endure a mental burden. The components are connected to producing more satisfaction at a later date.

3) Mood Management

It deals with the psychological ability to stay composed in any situation. It also gets rid of the stress that comes about in daily life. With the proper ability to manage your mood, you can also control feelings of sorrow which gives you the capability to settle disagreements with any grievances.

4) Motivational Factor

Those of us who have the capacity to motivate yourselves will possibly be more creative and efficient in all circumstances. Luckily, there are a large number of possibilities in which you can choose to create motivation. For instance, you can research the emotional intelligence benefits on motivation by studying books, keeping your goals in focus, assessing yourself and furthering your introspective awareness.

5) Social Skills

By possessing good social skills, people can create and foster relationships with anybody, through the use of emotional intelligence. Individuals with advanced social skills can interact with others in a delightful and tolerable manner.

6) Understanding People

The ability to understand other individuals with a level of appreciation is the vital element of emotional intelligence. It would be known as having a sense of empathy for others. The benefits you receive through understanding other people will allow you to build better relationships and communicate with ease.

Chapter 2
How Emotional quotient effects emotional intelligence

Emotional Quotient, or EQ, can sometimes be misinterpreted as Intelligence Quotient, or IQ. But there is a notable difference between the two. EQ measures your emotional intelligence, whereas IQ calculates your standard information. Emotional Quotient is the capacity to become aware of, comprehend and efficiently implement your position of emotions and feelings. It, in turn, simplifies high states of cooperation and productiveness. On a professional level, EQ is relevant because it assists you in influencing your recognition of emotions, leading to a more beneficial environment in your work area and with co-workers.

To accurately assess your unique emotional intelligence level, you will most likely take a test or answer a questionnaire to determine and score your EQ. It will then provide you with a detailed description of your score. As with any other test, the higher you rate, the higher your EQ is. Therefore, you will have a higher emotional intelligence level. No matter how high you score on the EQ test, you will gain a better understanding of what your emotional intelligence level is. It will prevent you from making any decisions that may be considered uncertain without first grasping how your emotions may be manipulating the choices you make. Rather than getting yourself in a bad situation, you can make a knowledgeable decision.

Emotional Quotient can show you a few different areas of intelligence to be conscious of within the scope of intrapersonal and interpersonal intelligence. Intrapersonal intelligence deals with the capability to recognize the emotional intelligence within you. Interpersonal intelligence is the competence to be able to grasp the emotional intelligence of other people.

Chapter 2
Increasing your EQ

Changing Your Perception and Mind

Emotional Intelligence is attributed to the power to recognize, analyze and regulate emotions, not only emotions in others but in yourself as well. While some believe that emotional intelligence is an innate trait, there are others who consider it to be a skill that can be cultivated and even strengthened over time. To increase your emotional intelligence or EQ, you must be flexible in your thoughts and beliefs. Emotional intelligence has an enormous impact on all facets of your life, including the manner in which you conduct yourself and how you connect with other people.

When you strengthen your ability to use emotional intelligence to your benefit, it will have a great impact on your everyday life. You will start to think more positively and become healthier, both mentally and physically. As your power to study and understand emotions increases, managing your emotions will become easier. You will find it simpler to deal with stress and eliminate it. Your communication skills will dramatically improve. Your ability to feel what others are going through will heighten. Challenges that present themselves to you will not seem like such a huge obstacle anymore. Through increasing your perception, you can also use that tool to being able to mediate arguments and disagreements between other people, and possibly yourself and another person. First, you have to change your perception and mind in regards to emotions.

Self-Motivation

Self-motivation is a power that pushes you to accomplish goals. It is operated by an enthusiasm for education, knowledge, and willingness to learn. By increasing your emotional intelligence, you will naturally want to improve yourself. Gaining the strength to grow comes from high self-motivation. It also lends itself to the desire to increase wealth and prominence, which are other forms of motivational factors. A higher level of emotional intelligence, about self-motivation, provides you with the ambition and obligation to carry out an endeavor. By increasing your self-motivation, you also gain the endurance to continue despite any hardships you may encounter.

Self-motivation is an essential ability to learn and master throughout life. If you would like to influence your personal growth, you cannot move forward without increasing your level of self-motivation. Comprehending and improving your self-motivation will assist you in the daunting task of organizing every other facet of your life. When you hold power to organize your life, you will most likely be more confident than those who do not place any value on self-motivation or growing their emotional intelligence. Self-motivation will provide you with fulfillment in your outlook on life.

Through the incorporation of a positive attitude, you can motivate yourself to achieve any goal you put your mind to. You have to train your mind to think in a positive light and rid yourself of any negative feelings. If these negative thoughts and feelings enter your thoughts, you will have the awareness to deal with them. You can turn them around and mold them into useful and purposeful feelings and thoughts. In turn, you will be able to reach your goals as your emotional intelligence pushes you to increase your self-motivation.

Learning about Others

In regards to emotional intelligence, you have to learn and increase your ability to decipher other people's feelings. This is known as having empathy for others. When you have empathy for other people, you will be more successful in life. As you improve your skills in determining how others are feeling, you will gain a better command over the nonverbal gestures you emit. Key factors that those with a high emotional intelligence have about experiencing empathy for others are defined in the following testimonies.

1) Business Adaptation

To improve your life, you also have to work on your emotional intelligence in the work setting. Your career is a large part of your life, so it stands to reason that you should place an adequate focus on it. It is important to predict and acknowledge what your employees, business partners, and clientele require of you. If you fail to meet their basic needs, you will struggle to maintain a positive outlook, not only in business but in life.

2) Enriching Others

When you exhibit a real sense of empathy, you will learn what other people need to feel better about their lives and themselves. You can assist them in meeting their personal needs and goals. As your emotional intelligence heightens, your feelings will be more in tune with the needs of others. Help them grow and become the active people they have their sights set on.

3) Creating Variety

As your sense of empathy increases, you can ascertain what the positive qualities are from different types of people. This will give you the ability to develop favorable circumstances by bringing out the best qualities of other people.

Understanding other people is necessary to successfully gain respect from your peers, in business and everyday life. After a while, you will acquire a sense of loyalty because you have fostered your emotional intelligence through the empathy for others. So how, in fact, can you improve your sense of learning more about others?

1) Hear the viewpoints of others. If you put yourself in another person's shoes, then you can more easily support certain positions. Even if you are apprehensive at first, move past those feelings and honestly try to see how the other person feels about something. It will be beneficial in understanding how people emotionally react to certain situations.

2) Take notice of body language. Body language plays a vital role in understanding the feelings of other people. If you aren't paying attention to how they are moving their arms, their eye movements when they speak or whether or not they are shifting on their feet, then you might miss the hidden tones behind what they are saying. You will not be able to grasp the feelings and emotional characteristics of others. If you show that you aren't paying attention, then you might lose a sense of trust you have with other people.

3) React to feelings. It resembles the ability to understand body language. If you know the hidden tones in speaking, you will be able to get a better grasp on other people's emotions. If someone contradicts their feelings with what they say and how they say it, then you can control situations more effectively. You will be able to put a positive spin on things. Show others that you do see how they are feeling and can nurture those feelings.

Learning Skills

Learning more skills to make your way through life is an important aspect of increasing your emotional intelligence. A good set of social skills provides a background for a skillful communicator. A key to developing these skills is to be open to both good and bad news. For circumstances where there happens to be bad news, you will be able to put a positive spin on things.

Those who possess exceptional social skills are known to control change and be able to find solutions to disagreements. If they are presented with an unsatisfactory situation, then those who have the emotional intelligence of proper social skills will feel dissatisfied in harmful atmospheres. Instead of changing everything themselves, they find it necessary and important to teach others how to improve their disagreeable conflicts.

Competence

Emotional intelligence is an awareness in everyone that feels somewhat abstract and hard to grasp. Some people have more difficulty than others in their ability to achieve a higher level of emotional intelligence. Emotional intelligence influences the way in which we control our behavior, maneuver in social situations and decide personal goals.

The competency levels make up a particular model on the subject of emotional intelligence. They are broken up into different categories. These groups deal with the self and social recognition and regulation of emotions and feelings. When you are speaking of the competence level of emotional intelligence, four first skills fall under two main competencies: namely personal and social competence. In a certain sense, they all tie into each other and cannot function as a well-oiled machine without one part or the other missing.

1) Personal Competence

It deals with how aware you are of yourself. It also includes your ability to maintain and regulate your skills set of emotional intelligence. These areas deal more with you, as an individual, rather than how you interact and get along with others. Personal competence keeps you mindful and knowledgeable of your different feelings and emotions. It also allows you to control the manner in which you conduct yourself.

Self-awareness – This allows you to be able to identify and understand your feelings as they are occurring meticulously. You also have the ability to keep them in your thoughts as you continue to your day.

Self-management – This is your ability to practice perception and understanding your feelings. It allows you to remain flexible and guide the manner in which you conduct yourself in a positive light.

2) Social Competence

Social competence is comprised of your social consciousness and the skills needed to manage relationships. It also includes being able to recognize how other people are feeling through their dispositions, demeanor, and intentions. You are using your emotional intelligence to develop the status of your relationships into more beneficial and active connections.

Social awareness – This provides you with a sense of being able to correctly recognize and decipher the emotions and feelings that other people are displaying, whether they are verbal or nonverbal cues.

Relationship management – This deals with your ability to pay attention to your feelings and emotions. You also have to incorporate other people's feelings to regulate communications between you and other people favorably.

How to Handle Stress

With a view to increasing your levels of emotional intelligence, it is wise to comprehend and have control over your emotions and feelings. It would be beneficial to your life as you try to accomplish the daunting task of recognizing and understanding stress. You learn to establish essential skills to govern and overcome all sorts of stress levels and allow you to become a great conversationalist.

Emotional intelligence is constructed by decreasing stress levels, concentrating and growing connection to yourself as well as other people. It is imperative to learn a few critical methods to do this.

1) **Lower stress during any time, place or atmosphere in a hasty manner.**

As it is occurring, you need to learn how to rise above your levels of stress in any given situation to function well. Recognize when you are stressed through your feelings and emotions. Establish how you will respond to stress so you can be prepared for high-pressure situations in the future. Determine what techniques work best for you, personally.

2) **Understand your emotions and don't allow them to take over your thoughts.**

Learn what type of relationship you and your emotions share together. How do your feelings come to you? When you have strong feelings, do you also have strong physical feelings? Do you scrutinize your emotional level?

These first two factors deal with the ability to oversee and delegate issues that are overwhelmingly stressful.

3) **Emotionally connect with other people through nonverbal gestures.**

To improve communication levels with other people, show them that you are interested and focused on what they have to say and with the projects they are working. Eye contact is forever important in having a meaningful conversation with anybody. Don't forget about nonverbal signals, such as how they are holding their arms and any slight facial expressions, as you are conversing with them.

4) **Remain associated in difficult circumstances by making light of the stress.**

Being flexible in how you react to stressful situations is okay. Don't be afraid to use a little humor to create a less stressful atmosphere. Loosen up and calm down during any situation that might get too stressful.

5) **Confidently positively settle disagreements.**

Concentrate on being in the present moment. You will be able to focus on any high-pressure situations as long as you are not always regressing to the past. Decide what is worth fighting for and what is not. You don't have to create an argument out of everything.

These last three skills have the ability to improve communication with other people significantly.

If you would like to change an attitude in a positive way that can continue under stress, you need to understand how to overcome this fear quickly. You have to stay emotionally mindful in your relationships comes through lots of practice and daily experiences.

Chapter 3
Developing emotional intelligence in the Workplace

Studies have shown that people with higher levels of emotional intelligence are more successful in the workplace. The reason for this is because these people have highly developed interpersonal skills that allow them to motivate, inspire, and relate to their coworkers. Emotional intelligence allows a person to diffuse arguments between workers while reducing stress and tension among those around them. These types of skills will enable you to climb the ladder quickly and show that you have the ability to manage a set of people in a business environment actually.

Every business needs to address how well the people that are part of the firm work with one another. Emotional intelligence at work is all about relationships and how they function. These links include worker to worker, management to management, management to worker and employees to customers and vendors. If there are rifts or issues in any of these areas your business won't be as successful as it could be. It's also important to see any problems that begin to form in advance before they become bigger problems down the road. Many companies fail each day because the people who work there don't have the interpersonal skills to keep the business moving forward and running smoothly.

Businesses that are emotionally intelligent have staff who remain aligned with your business ideals, are committed to the firm succeeding, productive, motivated, efficient, happy, confident, and likable. Remember, emotional intelligence can be applied to every type of person to person interaction that occurs in the business. From customer service to keeping staff motivated and willing to work, emotional intelligence plays a vital part in the day to day success of any business.

So that brings the question, how can we develop emotional intelligence in the workplace? Let's look at it from the both the employers and employees perspectives.

From the employee's perspective, employees are looking for jobs that they're passionate about and that take advantage of their talents. Employees want their employers to be mindful of who they are and what they need. Employees today aren't like our parents who mainly viewed jobs as a paycheck. They want a career they can be excited about and grow with. If an employee doesn't feel their employers care about these things, they'll be less engaged and less productive.

From the employer's perspective, management can be more efficient when they provide an environment that fosters, employee engagement, productivity, and teamwork. If an employer is too focused on their gain and not the needs of their staff, they'll suffer in the long run. Employers should have a management team filled with capable mentors who are committed to helping the other employees navigate the workplace and become better versions of themselves. Management needs to realize that everyone is different and therefore needs to be handled in a way that gets the most out of them. That is why emotional intelligence is so important. Being able to recognize who needs what and when is an incredible skill to have at one's disposal.

When it comes right down to it, business leaders need to be emotionally intelligent to be more efficient and effective at achieving desired results and maximising all outcomes. Employees need to be more emotionally intelligent with a view to work their way up the ladder and achieve the job and success they desire.

Here are five different ways employers can lead using emotional intelligence to help boost employees productivity.

1. Show That You Care About The People Around You. Caring about others is a simple thing you can do. However, it needs to feel genuine in both tone and delivery. Management should always remember to balance what their mind says with what their heart says. In work terms, this means you can't always be intense and overbearing about what you require out of your employees. Intensity works but only when used in the right way to keep or build momentum on a project. By being more compassionate and caring you'll show your workers that the job they're doing for you is being appreciated. Employees don't want to feel like a cog in the machine. They want to feel valued and appreciated. You don't need to babysit them or hold their hand, just let them know when they've done a good job and remind them of what things are expected from their job performance. If you do this properly, people will perform at a higher level.

2. Help Your Employees Feel Significant. Management should always try to be motivating their employees by showing them how their job benefits not only the company but their personal life as well. In today's society, employees want to feel like they're making an impact, which they're leaving their mark. Give them ways that allow them to feel this way, and they'll produce much more. When an employee gets a taste of success, they'll be willing to work harder to maintain it or surpass it.

3. Embrace People's Differences to Generate a Big Difference. In today's world, people's differences are very apparent. People like to feel authentic and will appreciate an employer who embraces those differences. By being sensitive on how you leverage and manage your employee's differences, you can assemble an excellent team that has people with unique talents, abilities and worldviews working together towards a unified goal. When conflict arises within a team, look for any similarities between the people to help you in resolving the dispute. By viewing differences as opportunities, you're putting your company in a better position to succeed. The more you include people that are different, the more the opportunities around you will grow.

4. Be As Accountable As Your Employees. Although management is in charge, it doesn't have to mean they're not viewed as equals with their employees. It means as management you need to hold yourself just as accountable as a regular employee, enforcing the same rules on yourself that you'd expect your staff to follow. Employees appreciate it when their leaders are open and available. They want to feel like an integral part of the team. They don't want to view it as management versus employee.

If management does something that is wrong, they should be transparent about it and admit the mistake. Employees want to see that their leadership can be trusted. Doing so will make you more genuine and real in their eyes. Employees will support and follow management that is easy to approach and easy to relate to. They want the control that will get in the trenches when necessary and fight alongside them. Management being accountable defines their real intentions. The more you are accountable, the more your employees will end up trusting you.

5. Always Be Mindful Of Your Employee's Needs. If you notice that your employees are not reaching their potential, or that productivity has decreased, you're doing something wrong as their leader. You need to be sensitive to your employee's needs and realize when there are issues that need to be addressed. Everyone can increase and improve their levels of productivity and performance. These improvements will only come with continuous feedback, suggestions, and recommendations on your part. If you're not holding up your end as management how can you expect the employees to hold up theirs?

A team is always stronger than its parts. However, you need always to be guiding your team for it to sustain and improve its level of performance. Get the most out of your employees by becoming mindful of any needs they have. Figure out what each employee needs to continue maturing and growing in their assigned job.

Employee Assessments

You may also want to try and get your staff professionally evaluated. The ESCI (Emotionally and Social Competency Inventory), is the only evaluation and development tool worked on by the leading authority of emotional intelligence Daniel Goleman. This study offers a 360-degree view of your employees and is more efficient than usual emotional intelligence tests that can be skewed by the user. If you want to assess your team properly, then this might be the way to go. Here is a *link* where you can check it out and see if it's right for your company.

Another solution is hiring people with high EQ, to begin with. Doing this will set you up for success from the outset. Many people feel this is the better approach than trying to improve the emotional intelligence of your current staff. However, I've seen both methods be effective when used correctly. Some employees will thrive when you help them develop a higher level of EQ while others will resist change and may need to be let go of in favor of someone who has the qualities you're looking for. I think the best approach is a healthy mixture of bringing in new people with the proper motivation, mindset, and desire while still trying to develop your current employee's EQ.

Whichever way you choose to get there is up to you and your business. In the end, what matters is that you have an emotionally intelligent group of people working for you that will achieve a maximum level of effectiveness and put you and your company in the best position for long-term success.

Developing Emotional Intelligence & Interpersonal Skills in Social Interactions

When talking about emotional intelligence the term "social skills" is made about the types of skills one needs to influence and effectively handle other people's emotions. To some, this might seem like a kind of manipulation, but it's not. Instead, it simply understands our own and other people's body language. For example, I now that when I smile at someone their naturally going to smile back, which in turns makes them feel more confident. There are times when this doesn't work or have the intended effect, but I've found it to hold true in general.

In this section, I'm going to discuss some of the different social skills and how they relate to our emotional intelligence. The goal of this chapter is to give you an understanding of the skills you'll want to improve on to raise your EQ level.

Building Rapport

Being able to build understanding with the people around you will make communicating much easier. Building rapport can happen. Naturally, some people just get along well from the outset; this is often how strong friendships are forged. On the flip side, you can build rapport with someone by finding some common interests and shared experiences. By actively listening and being empathetic you can develop a bond with almost anyone.

Learning to build rapport is an important tool to have at your disposal. Emotionally intelligent people can connect with the people around them by utilizing this skill. It's important in all forms of social interaction from work to personal life. Being able to get along with people will take you farther in life than if you're distant and unavailable.

Relationships are easier to have and maintain when you've developed a sense of understanding between both parties. For some people, it can be stressful to meet and engage with new people. Small EQ people will often have awkward body language and a difficult time starting or holding a conversation. If you fall into this boat, don't worry there are steps you can follow to get better in these exchanges. Try to stay calm and relax. The more you practice building rapport with people the better you'll become at it.

Conflict Management

Conflict and disputes are a part of life. In this section, Conflict often arises when people start to feel added stress, the anger of a situation they deem unfair, or from the loss of something or someone important. Learning how to manage these situations effectively and efficiently requires a higher level of emotional intelligence.

The unresolved conflict has been shown to lead to serious health issues as the added stress damages your body, leading to higher blood pressure and even heart attacks. That's why learning to deal with our conflict constructively and positively is important. It will not only improve your health, but it will improve your relationships in the long run.

Chapter 4
Awareness and understanding of the emotions of others.

Empathy- Practice Empathizing with Yourself and Others

The way we interact with other people often determines how successful we are in our career, in being able to diffuse conflicts and tackling challenges. Empathy is of utmost importance to be able to handle tricky situations with people and build lasting rapport. It involves the ability to understand the emotional state of someone else and treating that person according to his emotional responses. Ways to improve empathy include observing both verbal and nonverbal cues when listening to a person, such as the inflection and tone of the voice, posture, and gestures a person might make when talking. Hence, we are better able to decipher the emotions of the individual and deal with them efficiently.

One of the most significant skills you can master is the ability to improve your level of empathy. Our world expands too much time pointing out the imperfections in people. Empathizing with others can be something soothing in the lives of individuals. It will assist you and other people to live a rewarding and more active life. Here are just a few ways in which you can begin your journey of practicing empathy.

1) Listening plays a vital role in your ability to demonstrate understanding to others. You are giving other people your full and undivided attention, which can be a hard aspect to master in this day and age. Honest listening demands you to be in the present moment. You should not be wondering about things in the future or ponder on moments from the past. It is important that you keep

eye contact with the people to whom you are listening. It lets others know you are paying attention to them.

2) Make your feelings accessible. To connect with someone else, you should open yourself up, so your feelings and emotions are shown. You don't want to appear cold and uncaring. When you allow yourself to become somewhat vulnerable, you can build a deeper connection with other people.

3) Open up to physical affection. It is a sensitive step, and you should not just throw yourself onto other people. It is best to request the permission of the person you are willing to provide any physical affection to before you go ahead and initiate it on your own. Some people may be bothered by certain levels of physical affection and may not want to be touched. If you are speaking with someone you are very close to, then you can only give them a comforting hug or put your arm around them.

4) Concentrate on your environment and the atmosphere you are in. What are the emotions, demeanor, and behaviors of other people telling you? Pick up on these social cues to gain a better insight into what is going on around you. Studies have proved that when you exhibit a sense of consciousness about your environment, then you are more inclined to empathize with other people.

5) Don't be quick to judge other people. It is a vital step when you are communicating with others and are trying to practice empathy. Try to put yourself in the other person's shoes to better understand the situation. You may discover that your first impression is inaccurate, which might lead you to have a false sense of who that person is.

6) Lend a helping hand. When you are empathizing with another person, you can show that you care if you offer to assist in improving the situation. It demonstrates that you are caring enough to stop what is going on in your life to help another person out.

Examine How Your Actions Will Affect Others

Do you have the power to cause other people to grin, be happy, upset or irritated? Most people understand that our words and actions affect others, whether it be positively or negatively. As a matter of fact, through our power of selection, the words and actions we use more often than not have a powerful emotional consequence.

An individual behavior such as smiling or embracing other people may cause them to have a sense of happiness and joy. However, another behavior on the other side of the spectrum could create a feeling of sadness in others. It's impossible to make people happy constantly. We should understand how our actions and behaviors may affect other people before engaging in any social situation. If we find ourselves in a place where we would not want to upset another person, then we can take the necessary steps to prevent it from thinking ahead.

There are ways in which we can make our actions positively affect other people. Individual personal goals that we create can also have a pleasant effect on others. If we decide to help a charity or take time out of our schedule to mentor a child, then these people with whom we are dealing will have a beneficial improvement in their lives. These instances, among many others, show how your actions and empathy for others will undoubtedly make other people related.

Another aspect to consider is determining the action or behavior that doesn't allow us to understand how these choices may affect other people. Is it because some people tend to be more self-centered? It could lend itself to relaying a negative or uncaring message to others without truly meaning to cause them hurt. Of course, other personality traits can have a less than desirable effect on other people and their lives.

One of the most difficult things to do is to figure out and comprehend how other people are feeling. To try your best in not disrupting other people's lives or creating any tension, you should ask yourself ways in which you can positively adapt to certain environments. The first place you should start this formidable task is with your family. Then you can move on to other people that are close to you in your personal and professional lives. To master this adaptation, you should implement your effective listening skills and an adequate amount of time.

Practice Responding, Rather Than Reacting

Reacting can appear to be a more guarded form of acknowledgment than a response. When we react to certain situations, it seems to be disadvantageous. If we are not comfortable with things that are said or certain actions, then we tend just to react. Our emotions and feelings play a primary part in our reactions.

If we observe a response, we automatically know what it is. Some people will purposely do and say things, knowing they will cause a reaction. There is an adverse effect when someone reacts as opposed to responding. We allow our emotions propel us further ahead without any thought to reasoning. We can seem to have a loss of control. When you react, it is understood as being scattered and sensitive. However, a beneficial aspect can be intensity and devotion. To make that a positive side, you need to focus on your strength and not make it come out unexpectedly.

On the opposite side, we have a response to an acknowledgment. Our response still partly has a form of inciting a stimulus. However, responding to a situation is considered to be more mindful than reacting.

A positive aspect of a substantial response is the ability to have an intriguing dialogue. There will be only a sense of positivity and courtesy. We can only learn, evolve and acknowledge from these situations. We will have the chance to be more open and willing to be more honest.

To practice being more responsive instead of reactive, then we have to implement our ability to be mindful of others. Mindfulness does not necessarily come automatically, so here are a few practices to respond more attentively.

1) Breathe

Pay attention to how you are breathing and maintain a steady level and moderate rhythmic cycle. When you concentrate on your breathing, you will be able to think more clearly. You can get rid of thoughts that make you excitable and anxious.

2) Bodily Awareness

The more you concentrate, the better amount of knowledge you will have towards your body. You can be in control of your emotions and actions. When you direct all of your attention on your physical responses, you can allow your body to fall into a more stable condition.

3) Clearing Away Anxiety

As you become more aware of yourself, you will be able to have better control and a stronger ability to release your worries and stress. You can be made more fixated on who you truly are and what kind of person you would like to be.

4) Increase Awareness

As you control your mental relaxation and power, you hear things more carefully and pay more attention to ideas that are spoken. When you are trying to prepare your response, you will be more in tune with your surroundings. It allows you to deliver a more thoughtful response.

Types of People and How to Handle Them

Throughout our lives, we come across different kinds of individuals who have varied emotional states and who react differently to particular situations. More often than not, we have to deal with other people and their emotional outbursts as well. Some of the types of people we encounter are listed below:

Pessimists and Chronic Complainers

Pessimists drain all the positive energy out of the other person. They have a very negative outlook on life which causes them to wallow in feelings of hopelessness and doubt while hindering the progress of a particular situation or the resolution of a problem. Moreover, they are associated with chronic complainers who consistently point out every deficiency and defect in objects or situations. They are always blaming circumstances or other people for their shortcomings and lament in pools of despair instead of finding ways to improve their conditions. The best way to deal with these types of individuals is to oppose their destructive energies with positive energies by being optimistic and providing practical solutions through a problem-solving approach.

Aggressive

Dynamic types of people are bossy and can go to any lengths to have their needs met. They are usually not satisfied with a refusal to their demands. They can also display violence if thwarted and contradicted. These types of people can be dealt with by showing an opposite type of behavior by being calm and tactful.

Sensitive and Passive

The sensitive nature takes every single situation and comments very personally. He often experiences a drop in self-esteem as he feels hurt by any criticism and advice. Moreover, passive people tend to delay decision making and wish to be the invisible people in the room who only follow orders. They have no desire to contribute to any conversation or situation around them.

A person should first and foremost be aware of his emotional state and be able to regulate his reactions. Self-awareness consists of the ability of somebody to identify his moods and emotions and understand the effect that they can have on another human being. Through self-awareness, a person can acquire the necessary perception to be able to control his impulses to act in any given situation. Self-regulation allows an individual to think carefully before saying or doing something. According to Daniel Goleman's books on emotional intelligence, a person should have empathy, which is the ability to understand the emotional constitution of other people. Empathy is the skill of handling people according to their emotional responses. It involves putting oneself in the shoes of the other person to understand what the individual is experiencing and to be able to offer concern and sympathy. At the same time, one should not be engrossed in the emotion of the other person or let himself be affected by the emotional state of somebody else.

Furthermore, another aspect of an emotionally intelligent person is highly developed social skills. This type of individual would be adept in mastering relationships while blending easily in groups and being able to expand his network effortlessly.

Chapter 5
Managing the emotions of others

How Does EQ Work in Relationships?

How we use our EQ (Emotional Intelligence Quotient) has a huge effect on our daily lives. It affects how we interact with everyone around us, how we handle our own emotions and how we react to emotions in others. Our level of EQ determines how happy and lucky we are in all aspects of our life and especially in our relationships.

When two people live together, it's so important to not only be aware of our own emotions but also how they affect our partner. We then need to know how to deal with these feelings.

Our EQ behavior is often picked up from our parents and passed on to our children even if we aren't aware of it. Knowing how to handle situations constructively ourselves makes us better role models for our children.

How well we interact with our teammates, bosses, and customers at work can play a huge role in the success of our careers. The more developed our EQ is, the more likely we are to move into leadership areas. Many companies have now implemented EQ programs as part of their staff development strategies.

What Happens If You Don't Have a Well Developed EQ?

We often also misinterpret the emotions of others because we attach the wrong meaning to them. Maybe your partner is in a bad mood, so you assume you have done something wrong when perhaps they have just had a bad day at work. So if you aren't aware of that, you may end up in a bad mood, too.

People with Asperger's Syndrome (a high functioning form of Autism) often lack the ability to detect the emotions of the people around them, and this may result in socially inappropriate behavior. They have difficulty forming close relationships as they don't know how to describe or share their emotions.

Can EQ Be Taught?

Although some research suggests that EQ is genetically related, most studies now prove that it can be shown through coaching and self-help. People with Asperger's often show a huge improvement in EQ tests after coaching in reading nonverbal skills and in responding to different social situations.

Everyone can benefit from this sort of training. Couples can strengthen their bond; parents can pass on the skills to their children and workmates can become a more cohesive team.

We can seek the help of professionals or work through one of the many programs available online. However we approach it, when we actively strive to acknowledge our emotions and then manage them effectively, we are setting ourselves up for more positive outcomes in life.

EQ At Home 1 – Couples

Would you like to improve the quality of communication between you and your partner? Really, who wouldn't? In every relationship, there is always room for improvement.

So what if I said that you don't have to go to couples' therapy? I can hear your resounding "Yes" from here. Well, all it takes is a bit of commitment from both of you and the willingness to improve your EQ (or Emotional Intelligence Quotient) together.

How Can an Improved EQ Help Your Relationship?

Being aware of the moods of your partner and knowing how to respond to them can have a huge effect on how well you get along as a couple.

For example, when your partner comes home from work and

starts snapping at you, you might feel that they are angry at you about something and you start to get better. However, if you stop and think about it, you realize that perhaps your partner has had a bad day at work. So instead of snapping, you ask your partner if they want to talk about it instead. Which of these options do you think would result in the better outcome?

Communication Is the Key

Communication is not just about words. Our body sends out all sorts of signals regularly. There are the obvious ones like yawning when we are bored or raised eyebrows when we are surprised. But each of us has our own set of more subtle cues, too. These could include tapping our fingers when we are nervous or a slight downturn of the mouth when we disapprove of something.

When we are in a settled relationship, we can start to take each other for granted and stop paying close attention to each other. If we are not communicating well, small irritations can quickly build up to major issues. Also, emotions are contagious, so if one of you is feeling frustrated or anxious, the other may soon start to feel the same way.

So What Can You Do About It?

The key is first to be able to define your own emotions. What exactly is it that you are feeling and what's causing it? Then do the same exercise for your partner. Try writing lists and then swap them to compare your responses. If your answers are vastly different, then you know you have some work to do.

It's not enough to recognize the emotions and triggers; you need to know how to manage them appropriately. If you are both in a negative mood, this can be a real challenge. At least one of you needs to step back and regain some perspective. Once you can separate your emotions from those of your partner, you have a better chance of guiding the situation into a more constructive place.

The best part about being aware of how quickly negative emotions can spread is that positive emotions work the same way. Try smiling or gently touching your partner's arm and watch the effect on him or her. Couples that can learn to encourage and inspire each other and respond to each other with enthusiasm will build the foundations of a long and happy future together.

EQ at Home (Parents)

EQ denotes Emotional Quotient, also known as Emotional Intelligence. It involves recognizing your feelings and the emotions of other people. An emotionally intelligent person is self-aware as he can identify his emotional state and understand the effects of his emotional responses to other people. A self-aware individual can better regulate his behaviors by pinpointing his impulsive reactions and forming a sound judgment about the situation before acting. Such a person can control the negative emotions he may experience and prevent his emotional state from being disrupted by harmful sentiments. Childhood is a very delicate phase in a person's life as it determines his attitude later in life. Parents should first and foremost be able to develop their emotional intelligence and teach their children to cultivate their emotional responses.

Some Emotionally Intelligent Ways in Which Parents Can Deal with Their Children Are Listed Below:

Thought before Action

If your child behaves in a particular manner that makes you feel angry or anxious, you should first be aware of experiencing anger or anxiety which has been triggered because of an external factor. You should dissociate yourself from the negative emotion and be able to think about how to deal with the situation using an impartial approach. A child often mimics the reactions of his parents and thus the way parents treat their children in such a situation matters a lot. In doing so, you will not let a negative feeling alter your emotional state and will think regarding providing an effective solution instead of having behaviors that are offensive and damaging.

Help the Child to Understand and Express His Emotions

After identifying and describing the emotions you are going through, you must be able to successfully communicate them to your child and make him understand the effect of his emotional reaction to another person's emotional state. You should teach him to recognize his feelings and reflect on why he is experiencing such sentiments. At the same time, you should let him know that you fully understand the way he is feeling and that you are helping him to realize the trigger for the change in his emotional state. You should teach him to thoughtfully evaluate his emotional reaction by assessing if his behaviors are counter-productive or not, and hence if the emotions he is experiencing are beneficial or detrimental to him.

Develop Empathy

Understanding consists of being aware of the emotional constitution of other people and being able to treat them according to their emotional responses. For example, if there is a fight among siblings, you should teach your children to identify the emotions of each other and encourage positive feelings like compassion, forgiveness, and care. A child should be aware that each person thinks differently, has a different view of things and thus may react in an entirely unique way. An individual who displays offensive behaviors should be dealt with using calmness and a lot of tact as opposed to using aggression.

EQ at Your Workplace (Social Responsibility)

According to Howard Gardner, a Harvard theorist, EQ (Emotional Quotient) is the capability of a person to understand other people around him, their motivations and how to foster cooperation with others. While an emotionally intelligent person can identify his emotional state and the effect of his emotions on other people, he can also control his emotional reactions and analyze a situation thoroughly before responding. At a workplace, we are exposed to individuals with varying mentalities, ways of thinking and reasoning as well as different emotional responses. We need to learn how to cope with these numerous types of people and not to let their emotional reactions affect our emotional state.

Empathy is a characteristic of a person with high emotional intelligence. It allows an individual to be able to comprehend the emotional constitution of another human being and treat that person according to the emotion he may be experiencing. It involves putting oneself in the place of other people and expressing compassion when dealing with them. Thus a person having empathy can better communicate with clients and colleagues while understanding the needs and requirements of those people. Moreover, developed social skills are of utmost importance in a workplace. They involve the ability to manage relationships efficiently and to build networks effortlessly. At work, it is imperative to sustain positive relationships with all colleagues because a favorable rapport with everybody will foster teamwork and enable prompt organization of resources to achieve targeted tasks.

Moreover, an emotionally intelligent person has internal motivation, that is, the drive to perform for the sake of personal reasons other than money and fame. This type of individual is perfectly in flow, that is, he has a clear goal and vision of the future and works towards that goal, but at the same time he is happy in the present moment and can enjoy life fully. He has an inner understanding of what matters in life and is committed to pursuing his goals with passion while emphasizing his personal development throughout.

Much of the time, we have to deal with difficult people and situations at work. Some people have very negative attitudes and always focus on problems rather than deploying their energy to find solutions. Such people are energy sharks as they deplete constructive energies out of a situation. These people should be dealt with by employing an active approach and encouraging them to develop their problem-solving skills.

Furthermore, some people display arrogance and have very aggressive attitudes towards other colleagues. They can also be insufferable "know-it-alls" and consider only their opinions and methods to be the right ones. You should address those people with much calmness and tact. On the other hand, some people are very passive and are reluctant to shoulder responsibilities while being incapable of making decisions. They merely follow orders and have no wish to contribute to solving a particular issue. You should encourage them to expand their horizons and to develop their confidence and analytical skills.

Chapter 6
Tips & Tricks to Improve Your Emotional Intelligence

1. Be open to criticism and feedback. Be receptive to learning how other people view you and use that information to make any necessary adjustments.

2. Take the time to sponsor and mentor employees that have earned it.

3. Make an extra effort to be polite and thank people. When people are at ease they will be willing to perform harder for you.

4. Identify how you feel at multiple times of the day. Make a mental note when something triggers a strong reaction from you. You can use this information to learn what things you need to work on.

5. Employees appreciate management who are willing to share their privileges and perks.

6. Be consistent with your behavior and how you treat others.

7. Show that you're a thoughtful person. People respond to this much more than you might think. It will make achieving your objectives and goals much easier.

8. I suggest practicing mindfulness in all facets of your everyday life. Being mindful of everything around you allows you to become extremely aware of your own feelings and the feelings of others.

9. Take the time to celebrate any positive emotions. You'll find if you take the time to recognize your positive emotions they'll begin to occur more frequently. This will allow you to have better personal and professional relationships.

Chapter 6

10. Show that you care about people. This gesture is stronger than you might think in enabling you to achieve your leadership goals and objectives.

11. Before you act. Take a moment to pause, acknowledge any feelings or thoughts, and then clear your mind.

12. Take one long deep breath before you respond to something or someone when you're emotionally fired up. This pause will allow you the time needed to gather yourself.

13. Try and be compassionate in everything you do. While you won't always be successful coming at things from this angle will make you more in tune with the feelings of those around you.

14. If you hit some type of setback, take a moment to step back and analyze what you can and cannot control the situation. If you can't control something, let go of it and move on. This will allow you to focus on the things you can control in order to make progress past the setback.

15. A good practice technique to use is when you have an issue take a moment to consider it and then write down two solutions to it. This will get your mind used to think about problems before instinctively reacting to them.

16. Take stock of your strengths and then try to use them more often to your advantage.

17. Take stock of your weaknesses and find a way to gradually improve on them.

18. Learn to sense your emotions in advance so you won't get surprised or overwhelmed by them.

19. Once you've learned to acknowledge your different emotions stop to ask yourself what can be done about them and come up with solutions.

20. Try and stop your low EQ habits. These include judging other people critically. This is a difficult one for most people. Another one is taking offense when people are critical of you. It's easy to get defensive, but it's not beneficial. You should be learning how to rid

yourself of the bad habits replacing them with habits that will benefit you mentally and spiritually.

21. When at work have a feelings board available for your employees. This can be a whiteboard only split into three parts of the days with a list of emotions. Have your employees mark how they felt during each part of the day and then assess how your staff was feeling and when they felt certain things. You can begin to observe patterns by doing this and create solutions to help ease any little negative points that may arise for a majority of the staff during certain parts of the day.

22. Remember your emotions aren't just feelings. Try and understand what the message is behind your feelings. This will allow you a greater understanding of yourself.

23. Create an environment of positivity around you. Start cutting out the influences that are negatively impacting you and replace them with ones that benefit you. Having a positive atmosphere will allow you to open up and grow as a person.

24. Model your behavior after other high EQ people. No need to blaze a new trail when a perfectly good one has already been created to show you the way.

25. Embrace new ideas, people, and experiences. These will all teach you and offer opportunities for positive growth. Use them to your benefit.

26. Look for the best in others and don't ever be ashamed to ask for help. People with high levels of emotional intelligence realize their personal limitations and are open to support and help the people around them.

27. Don't fear change. It's a natural part of life. Emotionally intelligent people accept that the world will throw a curveball from time to time. Having the ability to adapt means you can roll with the punches and look at change as a new opportunity instead of as something to be upset about.

28. Don't withhold intimacy from your loved ones. The more emotionally intelligent you are, the more open you are to sharing

Chapter 6

your whole self with those around you. Don't hold back out of fear. Instead, let the people you care about know the real you.

29. Be intellectually curious. Growth is life. Always be exploring and learning new things about the world and people around you. If you don't seek out knowledge you'll never be able to evolve as a person.

30. Put yourself in other people's shoes. Your viewpoint isn't the only one or even always the right one. Allow yourself a few moments to look at things in a new perspective. Doing so will allow you to come into any discussion with an open mind free of judgment.

31. Take responsibility for your own actions and feelings. If you do or feel something you're not proud of own up to it and try to do better next time. No one is perfect, everyone will stumble and fall along the way. Don't get down on yourself, instead look at it as an opportunity to learn something new about yourself.

32. Don't hold things in. Doing this isn't healthy and will cause you to eventually lose control of your emotions and blow up. Work through your issues as they come up.

33. Don't let other people dictate how you feel about yourself. You need to be confident in yourself and your abilities. Don't let other people's opinions determine your self-worth.

34. Practice conveying what you're thinking in a non-threatening manner. Be respectful of those around you.

35. Emotionally intelligent people aren't afraid to share the way they feel. Practice sharing whenever possible.

36. Check your ego. Be open to other people's viewpoints and opinions. Don't let your ego get in the way of connecting with others.

37. Don't give guilt trips to the people around you. If you have an issue deal with it head on. Don't dance around the problem. Be direct but not rude or inconsiderate. Let the people in your life know where they stand with you. Don't do things like slam the door or give an attitude.

38. Emotionally intelligent people don't believe in manipulating

others or resorting to mind games. Don't prey on the weakness or kindness of others. Treat people like you'd expect them to treat you.

39. You don't need to win your conversation or argument. It's not a competition. Be open to hearing their side and consider what they have to say. Don't invalidate what they're telling you because you aren't in agreement with them.

40. Don't hold your intellect over the people around you. If you're smarter or more informed on an issue don't lord the fact over those around you. Instead, be humble and if someone wants more information, share it with them without being condescending.

41. High EQ people are usually very well balanced individuals. They don't tend to be too optimistic or too pessimistic. Work on finding ways to keep an even keel even when faced with stressful or unpleasant situations.

42. Emotionally intelligent people aren't bogged down with things like fear, shame, guilt, obligation, and embarrassment. Work on facing the negative emotions and feeling comfortable in your own skin.

43. Work on becoming more present in your daily life. You can't control the past or the future. There's no reason to continue living anywhere but in the here and now.

44. Don't shut out the people in your life. Many low EQ people will seek a substitute relationship that they are able to control. This can be with other people, getting additional pets, or even creating fictional relationships. Deal with the issue, don't replace it with something else hoping your problems will disappear.

45. Learn to recognize your feelings. Feelings about something don't mean that something is a fact. Just because your heart says one thing doesn't mean it's true. High EQ people are able to separate their feelings from the reality of situation.

46. Give yourself the gift of meditation and silence. Allow yourself time to just be at the moment. I suggest doing this on a daily basis if possible.

47. Learn the benefit of denying yourself immediate satisfaction for long term gain. This can be either at work or at home. Don't sac-

rifice future goals, success and happiness just because a lesser option can be achieved now. Learn the value of saying no and waiting for what you really desire.

48. Learn to trust in your decisions. The more confident you become in your decision making process the more you'll be able to trust your intuition is guiding you the right way. High EQ people know when to trust themselves.

49. Practice humility. High EQ people don't see the need to brag or boast about who they are or what they are able to do.

50. Practice talking with new people in public settings. The more comfortable you get connecting with strangers, the more you'll begin to pick up on people's verbal and nonverbal cues going forward.

Conclusion

Emotional Intelligence enables you to recognize, manage and articulate your emotions. It also allows you to appreciate interpersonal relationships intelligently and compassionately. Over time, our work environments have become more and more involved and contested. Business owners are always faced with the challenge of engaging employees and competitive building advantages at a time when everything is changeable.

In all types of businesses, emotional intelligence smarts are viewed as urgently necessary and vital to running a business. In fact, many universal companies are placing a high value on emotional intelligence in their work crew which will guarantee a higher level of achievement in production as well as increase people's skills. Emotional intelligence continues to produce primary outcomes throughout different manufacturers and businesses. Research and studies that have taken place for an extended period have shown the effects of creating and gathering resources for emotional intelligence on management, employee collaboration, supervisory atmosphere, synergy, transactions and client fidelity.

P.S. I would be very grateful if you leave your feedback on the book, tell us what exactly helped you, share your story and thus help other people find the necessary information and support. Write a customer review

Sincerely, Anne Gilmore

All rights reserved.

No part of this publication or the information in it may be quoted from or reproduced in any form by means such as printing, scanning, photocopying or otherwise without prior written permission of the copyright holder.

Disclaimer and Terms of Use: Effort has been made to ensure that the information in this book is accurate and complete. However, the author and the publisher do not warrant the accuracy of the information, text, and graphics contained within the book due to the rapidly changing nature of science, research, known and unknown facts and the internet. The Author and the publisher do not hold any responsibility for errors, omissions or contrary interpretation of the subject matter herein. This book is not intended for use as a source of legal medical, business, accounting or financial advice. All readers are advised to seek services of competent professionals in the legal, medical, business, accounting, and finance field. This book is presented solely for motivational and informational purposes only.

www.ingramcontent.com/pod-product-compliance
Lightning Source LLC
Chambersburg PA
CBHW030519220526
45464CB00006B/2864